ROUNDABOUT
THEATRE
COMPANY

MW01485262

Todd Haimes, Artistic Director
Harold Wolpert, Managing Director
Julia C. Levy, Executive Director
Sydney Beers, General Manager

in association with

Amy Sherman-Palladino and Daniel Palladino   David Mirvish   Barry and Fran Weissler
Elizabeth Armstrong   Mary Jo and Ted Shen

presents

Sutton Foster

Colin Donnell   Alexander Gemignani   Joshua Henry

VIOLET

Based on the New York City Center *Encores!* Off-Center concert production

Music by
Jeanine Tesori

Book and Lyrics by
Brian Crawley

Based on "The Ugliest Pilgrim" by Doris Betts

with

Ben Davis   Annie Golden   Emerson Steele

Austin Lesch   Anastacia McCleskēy   Charlie Pollock
Jacob Keith Watson   Rema Webb   Virginia Ann Woodruff

Set Design	Costume Design	Lighting Design	Sound Design
David Zinn	Clint Ramos	Mark Barton	Leon Rothenberg

Orchestrations	Musical Coordinator	Hair & Wig Design	Dialect Coach	Production Stage Manager
Rick Bassett Joseph Joubert Buryl Red	Seymour Red Press	Charles G. LaPointe	Kate Wilson	Kristen Harris

Casting	Violet General Manager	Production Management	Press Representative
Jim Carnahan, C.S.A. Carrie Gardner, C.S.A. Stephen Kopel, C.S.A.	Denise Cooper	Aurora Productions	Polk & Co.

Associate Managing Director	Director of Marketing & Audience Development	Director of Development
Greg Backstrom	Tom O'Connor	Lynne Gugenheim Gregory

Founding Director	Adams Associate Artistic Director*
Gene Feist	Scott Ellis

Music Direction by
Michael Rafter

Choreography by
Jeffrey Page

Directed by
Leigh Silverman

Roundabout gratefully acknowledges partial underwriting support from Gina and David Boonshoft.

Playwrights Horizons, Inc., New York City, produced *Violet* Off-Broadway in 1997, and it was
initially developed at the O'Neill Theatre Center during the 1994 National Music Theatre Conference.

Original Broadway Cast Recording on PS CLASSICS.

*Generously underwritten by Margot Adams, in memory of Mason Adams.
Roundabout Theatre Company is a member of the League of Resident Theatres. www.roundabouttheatre.org

ISBN 978-1-4803-9677-7

 HAL•LEONARD®
CORPORATION

7777 W. BLUEMOUND RD. P.O. BOX 13819 MILWAUKEE, WI 53213

In Australia Contact:
Hal Leonard Australia Pty. Ltd.
4 Lentara Court
Cheltenham, Victoria, 3192 Australia
Email: ausadmin@halleonard.com.au

Visit Hal Leonard Online at
www.halleonard.com

SURPRISED

Music by JEANINE TESORI
Lyrics by BRIAN CRAWLEY

Colla voce

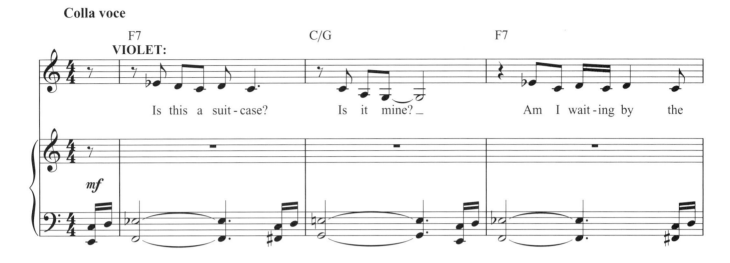

VIOLET: Is this a suit-case? Is it mine? _ Am I wait-ing by the

can-dy _ stand, _ be-neath the Grey-hound Sta-tion sign? _

Have I got a tick-et in my hand? _ Stu-pid, _____ the

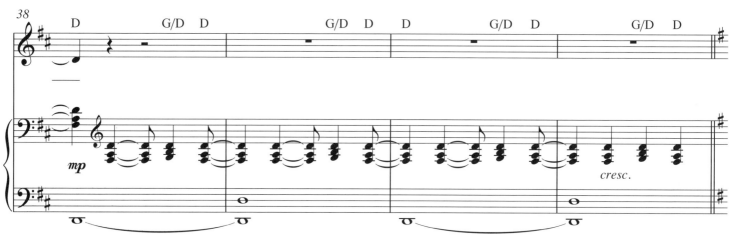

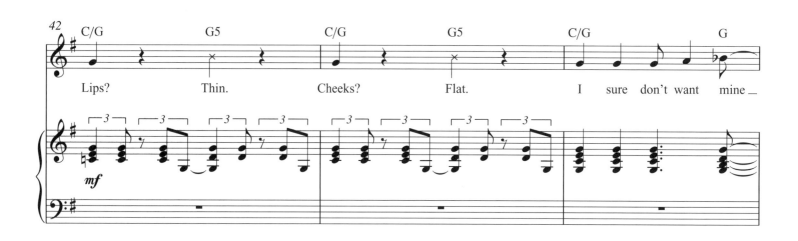

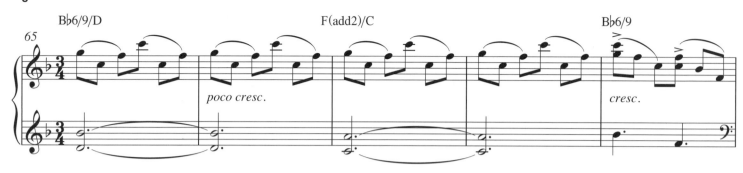

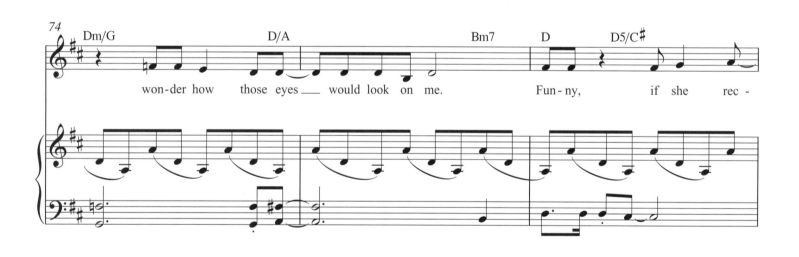

ON MY WAY

Music by JEANINE TESORI
Lyrics by BRIAN CRAWLEY

ALL TO PIECES

Music by JEANINE TESORI
Lyrics by BRIAN CRAWLEY

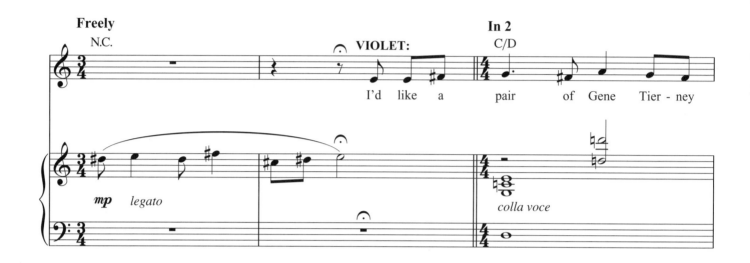

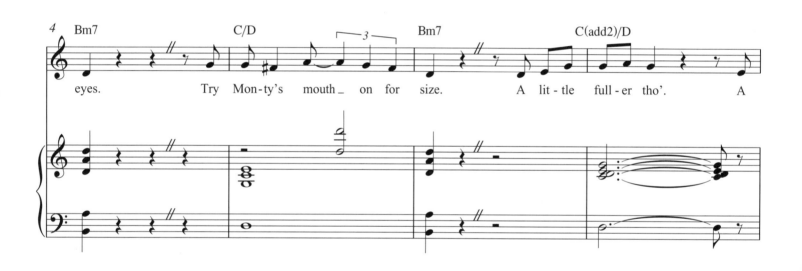

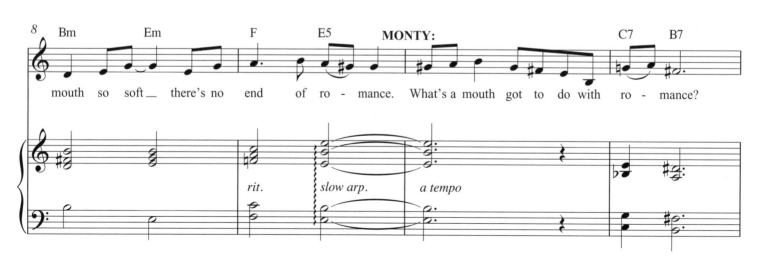

* *All sung on one pitch, ad lib.*

44
with lips like those, _____ I'd _____
one of Bar - dot's. _____ Why _____

48
look al - most shame - less. _____ Oh _____
should she be stin - gy? _____ Oh _____

G7

52
but add the nose, _____ now
throw in her toes. _____ Mine

56
I'm pure and blame - less. If Cyd Char - isse _____ is - n't
are just too din - gy. I'd give my preach - er my

A7

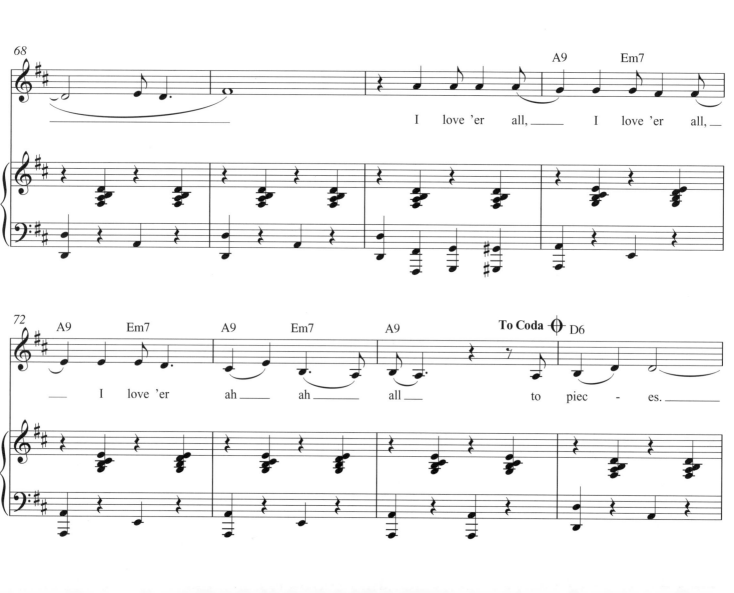

LET IT SING

Music by JEANINE TESORI
Lyrics by BRIAN CRAWLEY

Raise your foot, now that's the way. *(He slaps the rhythm on his thigh, ham-bone style)* You'll be mov-in' on to-day.

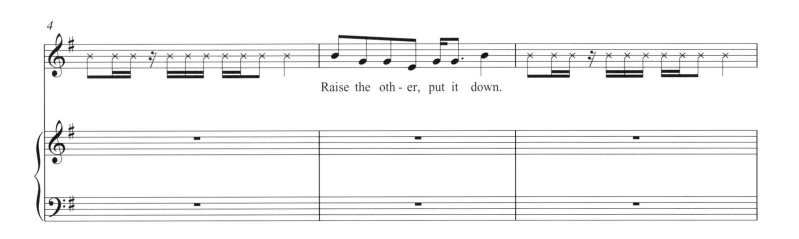

Raise the oth-er, put it down.

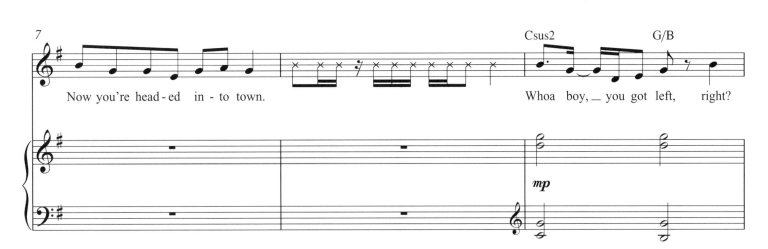

Now you're head-ed in-to town. Whoa boy, __ you got left, right?

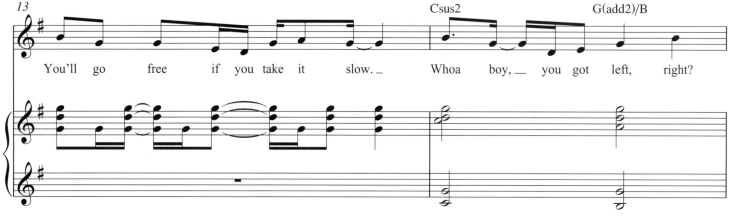

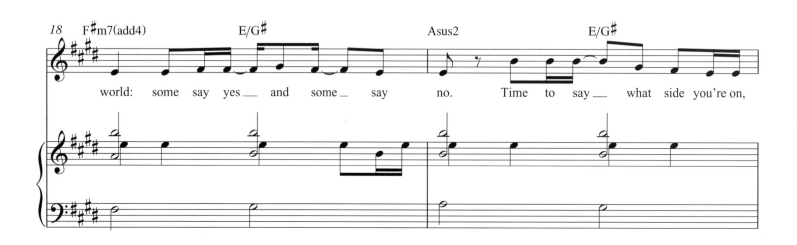

LAST TIME I CAME TO MEMPHIS

Music by JEANINE TESORI
Lyrics by BRIAN CRAWLEY

42

LAY DOWN YOUR HEAD

Music by JEANINE TESORI
Lyrics by BRIAN CRAWLEY

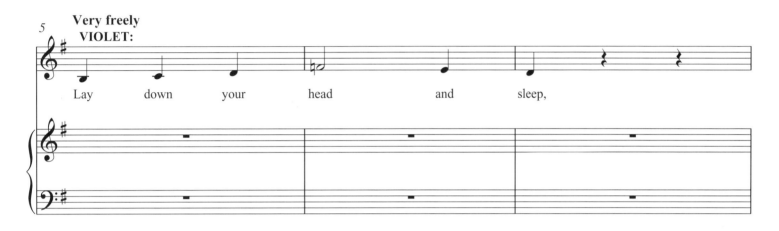

Lay down your head and sleep,

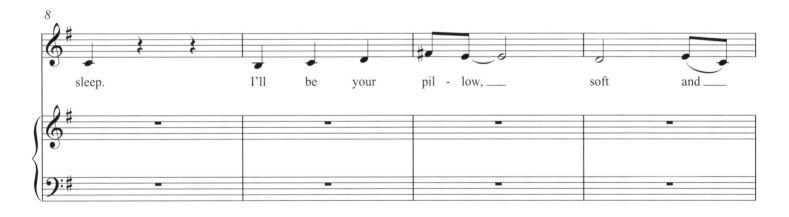

sleep. I'll be your pil - low,___ soft and___

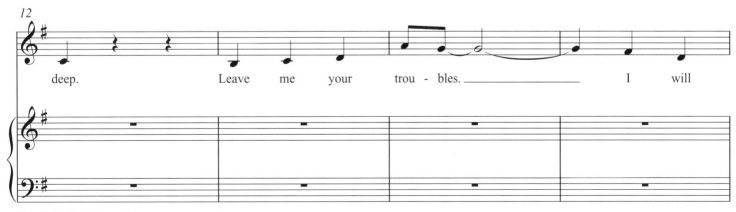

deep. Leave me your trou - bles._____ I will

Originally in A major.

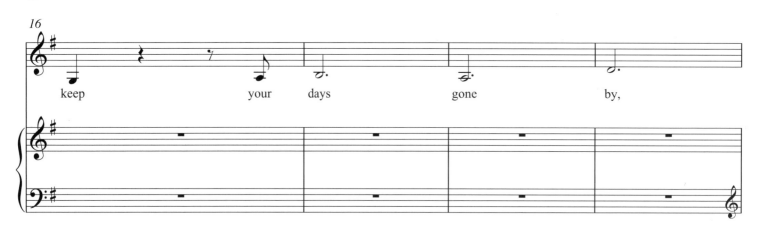

keep your days gone by,

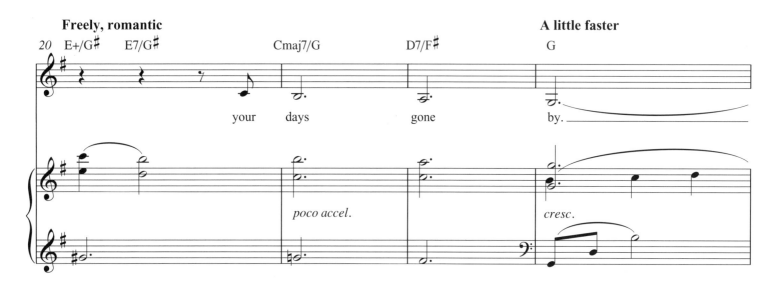

your days gone by.

Freely, romantic **A little faster**

your days gone by.

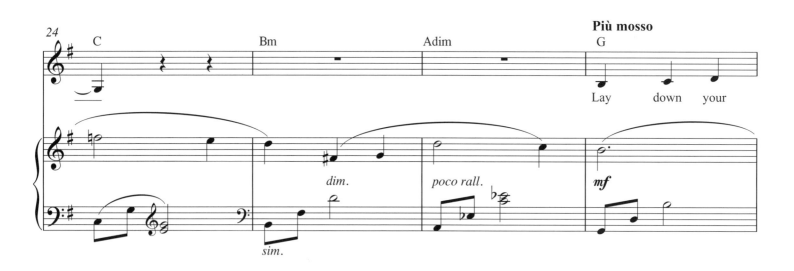

Lay down your

Più mosso

head and dream, dream. You're so much

Moving ahead

HARD TO SAY GOODBYE

Music by JEANINE TESORI
Lyrics by BRIAN CRAWLEY

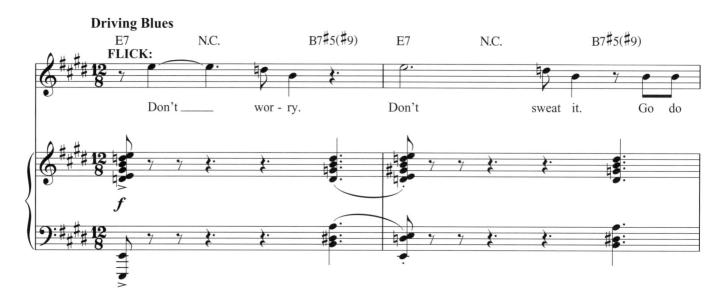

FLICK: Don't ____ wor - ry. Don't ____ sweat it. Go do

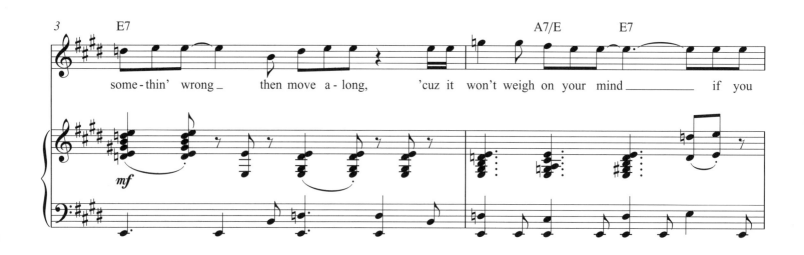

some-thin' wrong ___ then move a - long, 'cuz it won't weigh on your mind _____ if you

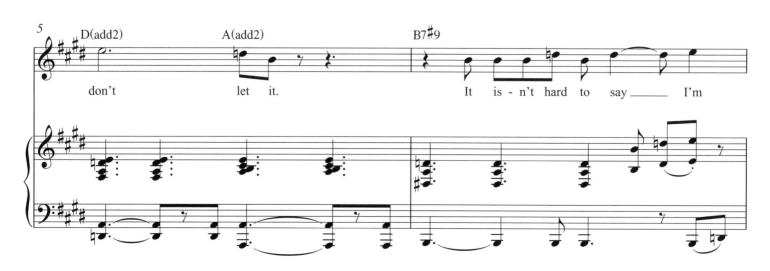

don't ____ let it. It is - n't hard to say ____ I'm

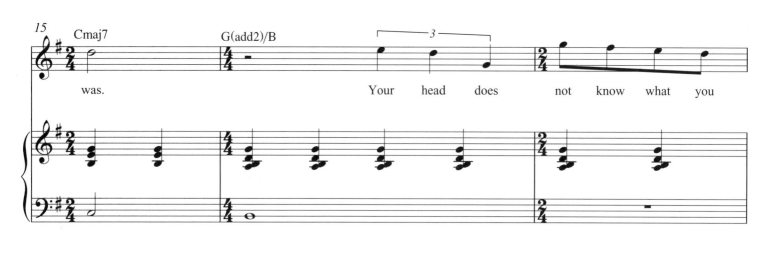

Driving Blues

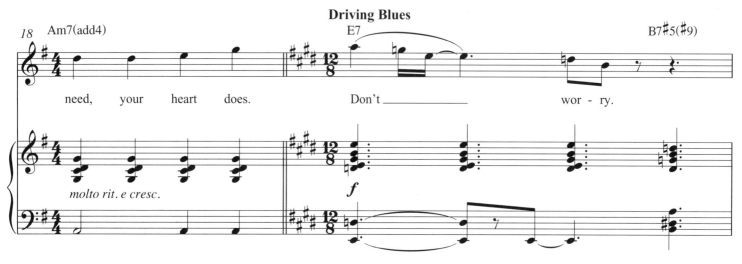

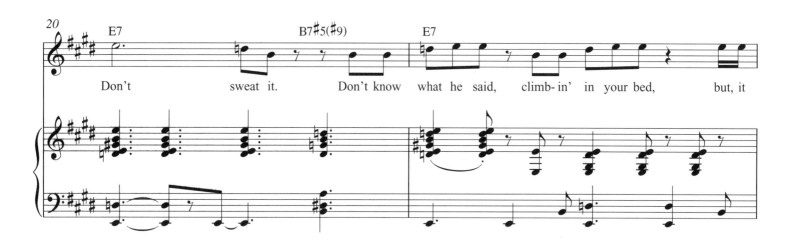

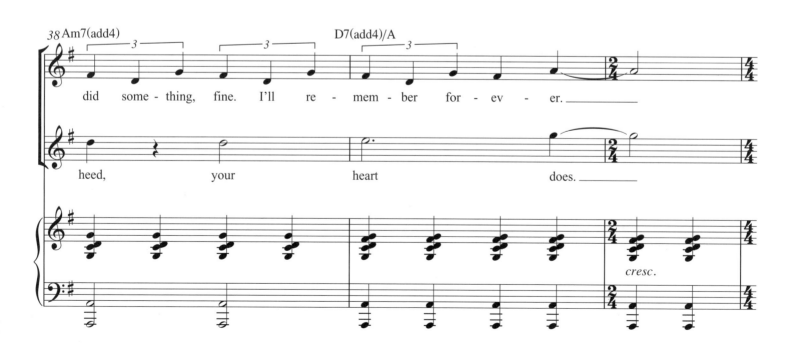

PROMISE ME, VIOLET

Music by JEANINE TESORI
Lyrics by BRIAN CRAWLEY

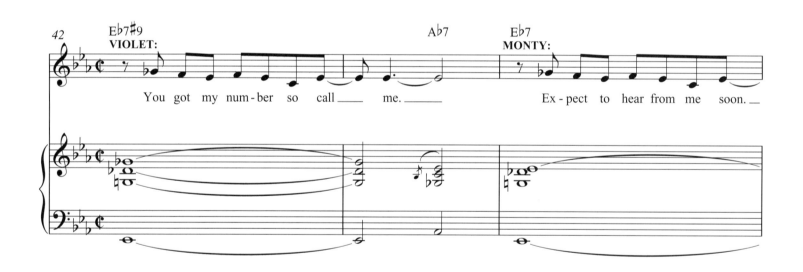

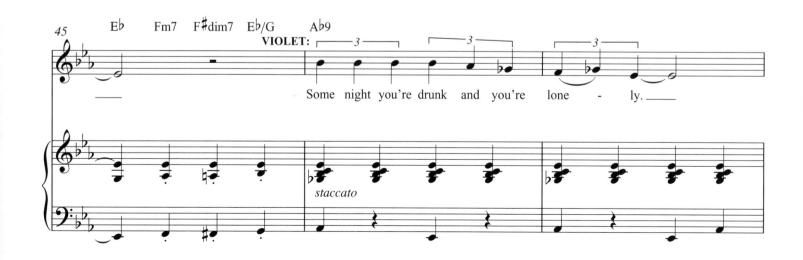

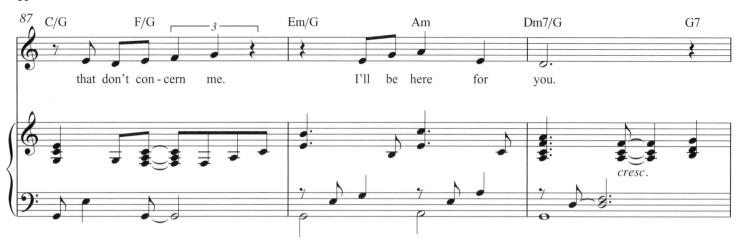

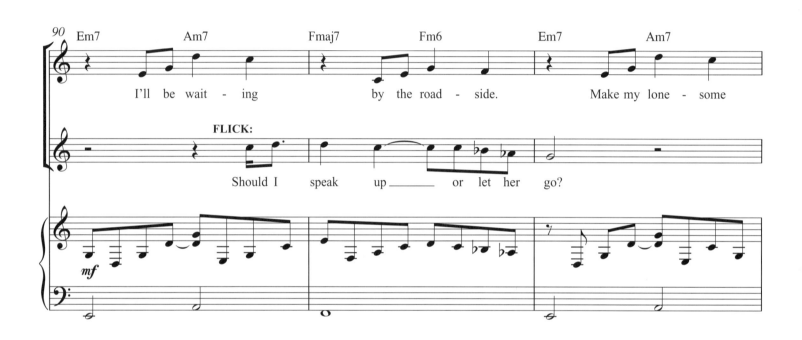

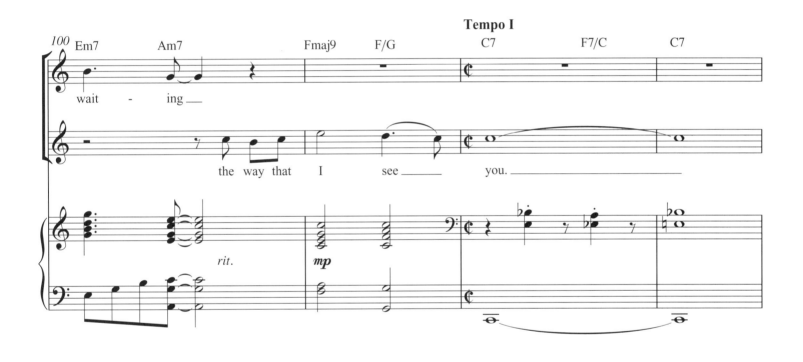

LOOK AT ME

Music by JEANINE TESORI
Lyrics by BRIAN CRAWLEY

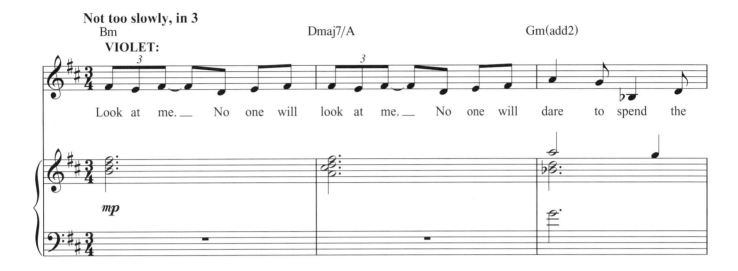

Not too slowly, in 3

VIOLET:
Look at me.__ No one will look at me.__ No one will dare to spend the

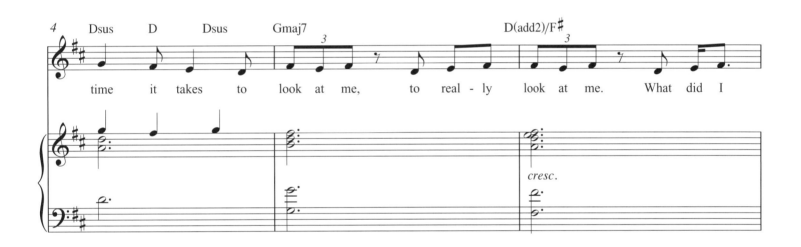

time it takes to look at me, to real-ly look at me. What did I

Agitato, in 1 (♩ = 164)

do to make you an-gry at me? My God,____

THAT'S WHAT I COULD DO

Music by JEANINE TESORI
Lyrics by BRIAN CRAWLEY

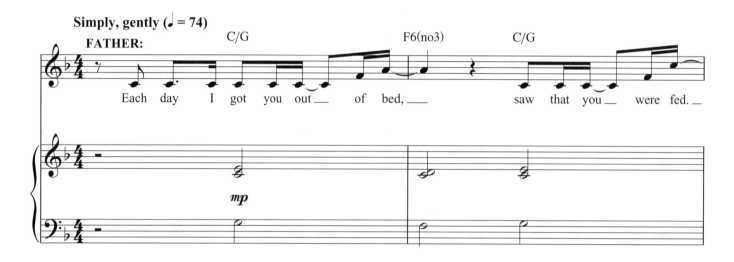

Simply, gently (♩ = 74)

FATHER:

Each day I got you out __ of bed, __ saw that you __ were fed.

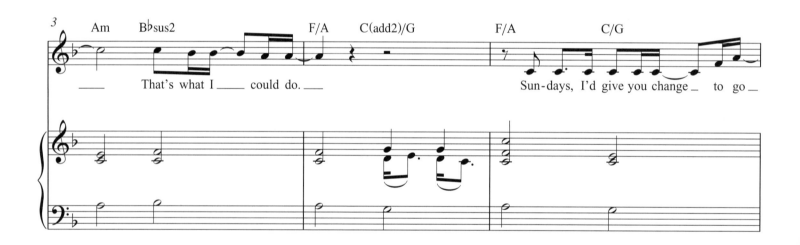

__ That's what I __ could do. __ Sun-days, I'd give you change __ to go

__ to a pic-ture show. That's what I __ could do, __ that's all I knew to

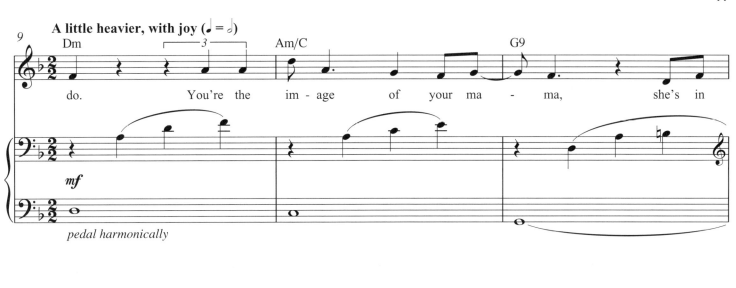

do. You're the im - age of your ma - ma, she's in

ev - 'ry - thing ___ you are. You've got her eyes, ___ you've got her smile. ___

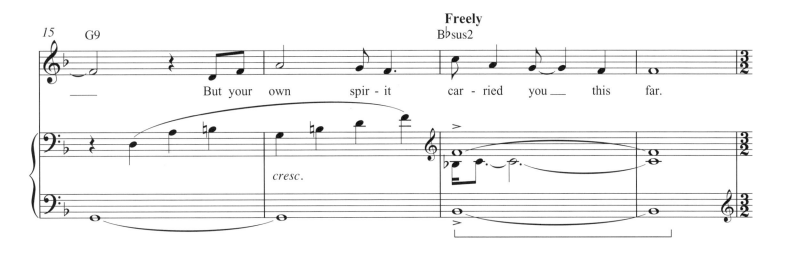

___ But your own spir - it car - ried you ___ this far.

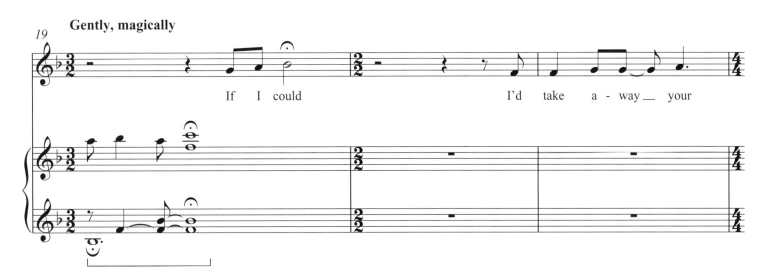

If I could I'd take a - way ___ your

BRING ME TO LIGHT

Music by JEANINE TESORI
Lyrics by BRIAN CRAWLEY

Moderate Pop Ballad

FLICK: If I ask you to be ___ with me by ___ and by, will you meet me to-night ___

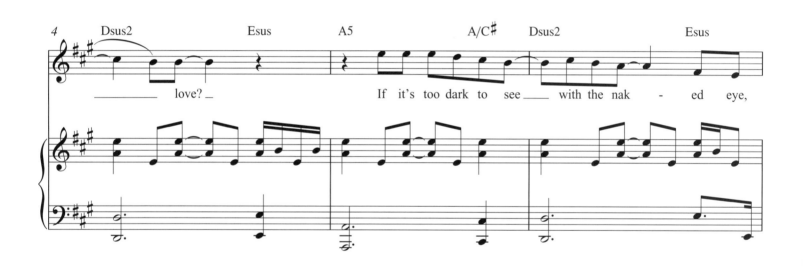

___ love? ___ If it's too dark to see ___ with the nak - ed eye,

will you bring me to light? ___ add VIOLET: If I hap - pen to stag-

a little heavier

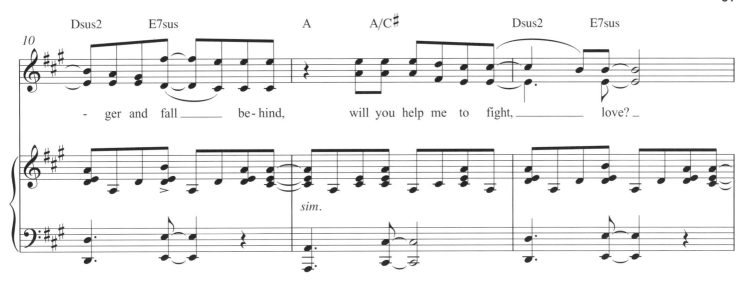

-ger and fall _____ be-hind, will you help me to fight, _____ love? _

Will you help me to walk, will you ease _____ my __ mind, will you bring me to light? _

add EARL:

add OLD LADY:

Will you bring me to light? __

cresc.

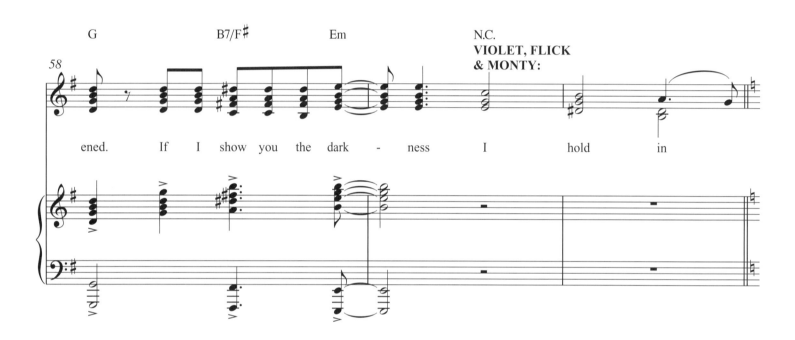

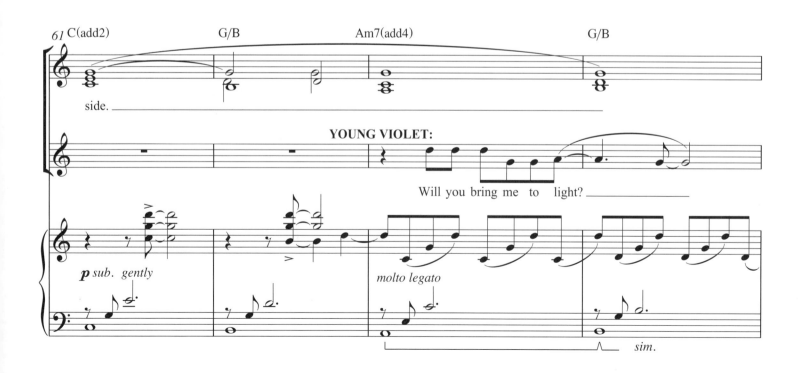

YOU'RE DIFFERENT

Music by JEANINE TESORI
Lyrics by BRIAN CRAWLEY

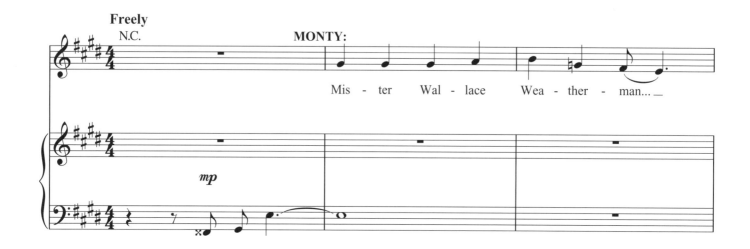

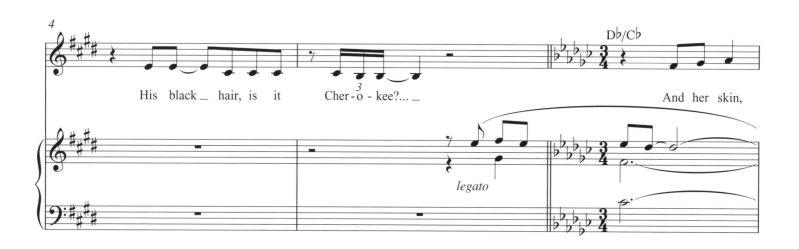

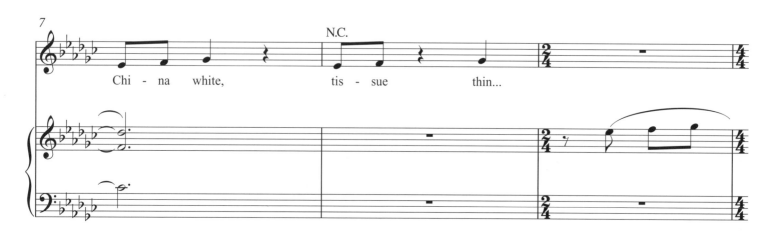

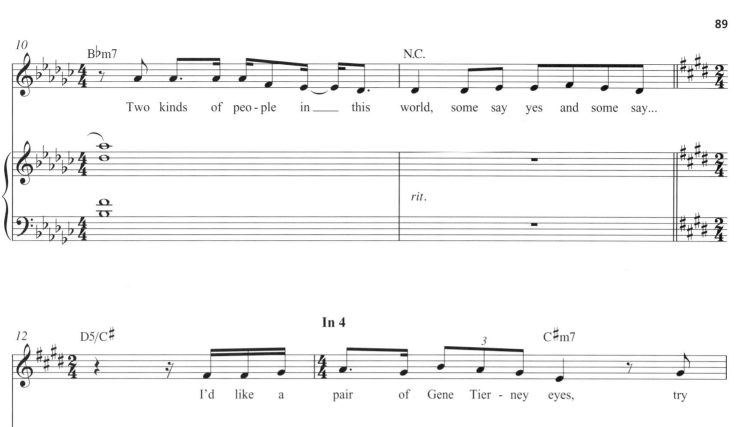

Two kinds of peo-ple in ___ this world, some say yes and some say...

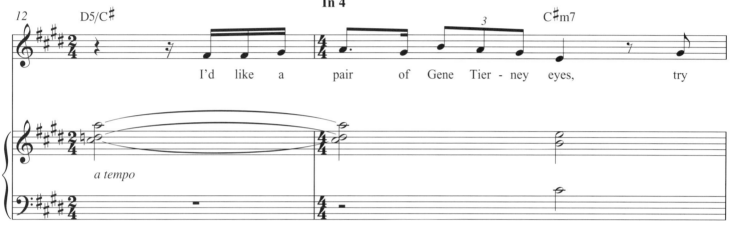

I'd like a pair of Gene Tier-ney eyes, try

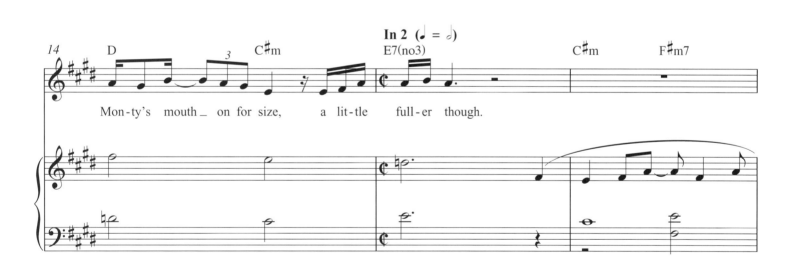

Mon-ty's mouth _ on for size, a lit-tle full-er though.

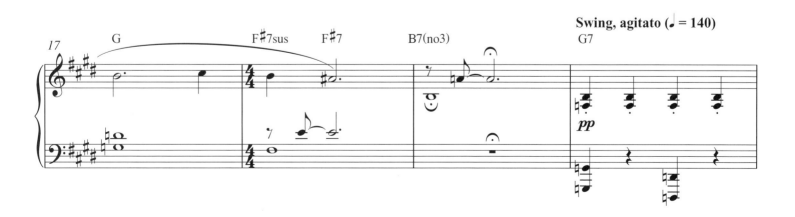

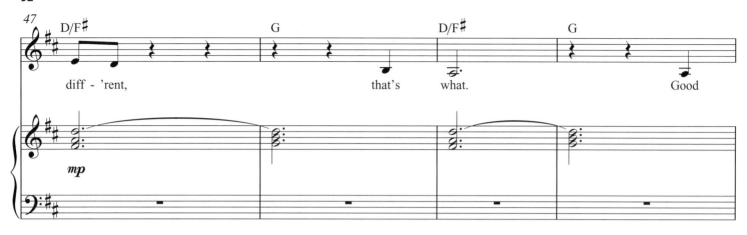

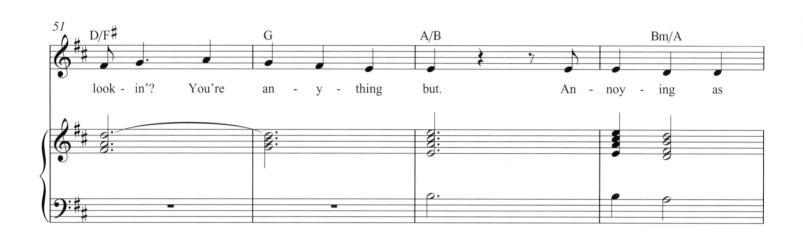

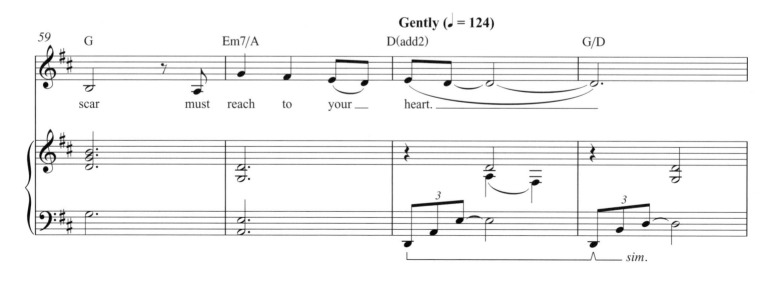